The Music Master

Puzzle Book

By

Graham Bennett

Author, Composer & Publisher

This book is dedicated to the enjoyment of learning the musical language

**The Music Master
Puzzle Book**

First Published 2005
by Egon Publishers

First Published 2008
by The Music Master Publications

Copyright © Graham Bennett
and The Music Master Publications

ISBN: 978-0-9559184-5-2

Printed for the publisher by
Howard Digital Limited
Business Centre West, Unit 5a, Avenue One, Herts. SG6 2HB

Contents

𝕿𝖍𝖊 𝕿𝖗𝖊𝖆𝖘𝖚𝖗𝖊 𝖔𝖋 𝕷𝖔𝖓𝖌 𝕴𝖘𝖑𝖆𝖓𝖉

If you are lucky enough to find this note and 'safe'………..

A safe was washed up on the coast of 'Long Island' in the Indian Ocean. Attached to it was a metal plate with a message engraved. It read…….

𝖂𝖍𝖔 𝖊𝖛𝖊𝖗 𝖋𝖎𝖓𝖉𝖘 𝖙𝖍𝖎𝖘 𝖙𝖗𝖊𝖆𝖘𝖚𝖗𝖊 𝖘𝖆𝖋𝖊 𝖎𝖘 𝖜𝖊𝖑𝖈𝖔𝖒𝖊 𝖙𝖔 𝖐𝖊𝖊𝖕 𝖙𝖍𝖊 𝖈𝖔𝖓𝖙𝖊𝖓𝖙𝖘 𝖎𝖋 𝖙𝖍𝖊𝖞 𝖈𝖆𝖓 𝖉𝖎𝖘𝖈𝖔𝖛𝖊𝖗 𝖙𝖍𝖊 𝖈𝖔𝖒𝖇𝖎𝖓𝖆𝖙𝖎𝖔𝖓.

On the top of the safe there was a little hatch which once opened revealed some papers. I think they might be clues to the combination…….

Can you solve the puzzle?????

There are six parts to this puzzle. The instructions are explained on each part.

Good Luck

Part One

To complete this part of the puzzle and collect the first clue to the combination, find all of the words below in the word search. As you find the words you will discover another word (a famous country). Complete the word and the letter which comes after this word is your first clue. (to help you.......think of a treasure map)

C	O	M	P	O	S	I	T	I	O	N	O	T	L	E
F	Z	M	G	M	J	Q	S	N	V	D	G	R	E	J
S	S	E	M	I	Q	U	A	V	E	R	U	K	G	F
I	K	S	C	H	S	B	R	B	P	L	S	H	E	T
N	O	T	E	H	H	L	M	Q	O	I	X	V	R	N
D	A	O	C	N	O	T	E	V	A	L	U	E	L	M
A	L	Y	Z	C	S	S	Y	P	W	Z	W	U	I	E
D	F	E	T	C	T	B	L	E	G	A	T	O	N	T
C	J	A	N	H	A	G	M	O	Z	A	R	T	E	S
E	V	I	E	T	K	L	X	K	V	I	V	A	C	E
E	M	T	P	R	O	W	A	T	T	A	C	C	A	T
Q	A	X	N	B	V	S	U	Z	A	V	K	D	B	O
C	O	Y	E	H	I	I	F	N	S	V	W	I	K	N
R	V	D	O	L	C	E	G	T	T	X	V	N	A	R
X	D	S	K	R	H	M	D	K	B	O	A	C	F	X

The first clue is

....

Legato

Attacca

Octave

Shostakovich

Note value

Note stem

Semiquaver

Lento

Vivace

Dolce

Legerline

Mozart

Composition

Mesto

Note

Part Two   ℱind the identical melody

To complete this part of the puzzle you need to find a melody which is exactly the same as the original. Is the next clue.......1, 2, 3, 4, 5, or 6? Circle the correct answer.

Answer:...

Part Three   𝕹ote value equations

First you need to complete the note value equations by adding or subtracting. When you have your answers add them all together. Divide this total with the 'last note value equation answer' and the final answer is the next clue to the combination of the safe.

Answer:..

Part Four

Composers and their nationalities

Composer	Country
Frederic Chopin	....
George Gershwin	....
Igor Stravinsky	....
Joaquin Rodrigo	....
Giacomo Puccini	....
Claude Debussy	....
Wolfgang Amadeus Mozart	....

For this part of the puzzle you need to research the composers above and find out which countries they came from. Then when you have all the countries take the first letter of each country and put them together. They start to spell the title of a famous opera. However the last letter of the name is missing.
To find the last letter look in a German dictionary for the word which means 'Song'. The first letter of this translation is the last letter of the opera name.

Once you have the complete name of the opera find out who wrote it. The last letter of the composer's surname is your next clue.

Answer:....................................

Part Five

ʜᴏᴡ ʟᴏɴɢ ᴅɪᴅ ᴛʜᴇsᴇ ᴄᴏᴍᴘᴏsᴇʀs ʟɪᴠᴇ?

Composer	Birth year	Death year	Age
Johann Sebastian Bach	....	....	......
Joseph Haydn	....	....	......
Johannes Brahms	....	....	......
Dimitri Shostakovich	....	....	......
Edward Grieg	....	....	......
Wolfgang Amadeus Mozart	....	....	......
Franz Liszt	....	....	......
Ludwig Van Beethoven	....	....	......

First you need to research and find out the year when each composer was born and then the year when each composer died. From these dates calculate how old each composer was when they died. There are two composers who died the same age. When you find them, add the two ages together and divide your answer by 4. The answer will provide you with the next clue to the combination.

Answer:..

6

Part Six

The Last Hurdle

1) How many movements does a 'typical' symphony have? ....

2) How many instruments are there in an 'octet' ? ....

3) How many symphonies did Johannes Brahms write? ....

To complete this part of the puzzle and complete the entire puzzle you need to answer the three questions above. Once you have the answers, add them together and then divide by 8. The answer is the last clue to the combination.

Once you have all of your answers from the six puzzle sheets compare them with the combinations below. Can you find the correct combination?

If yes... Well Done!!!!!!!

If no... go back and check your answers!!!!

Combinations to choose from:

X79A247	X79B439	U41B232	R29C438
X68C439	D56R322	Z41B394	G56D322
Y41A247	A51B232	X41B237	X41A247
Z68B493	M41B232	X56R322	Y79A247

Circle the correct combination.

7

Graham's word search

To complete this puzzle simply answer the 10 questions below and then try and find your answers in the word search.

M	A	L	Z	W	L	X	N	D	W	R	M	T	B	C
T	A	S	E	O	J	D	H	O	K	V	B	Y	E	I
V	A	Z	Y	V	K	R	W	G	C	R	D	Q	M	F
X	S	U	U	E	K	S	P	C	J	T	Q	B	U	U
M	A	L	Q	R	B	M	T	J	V	C	U	A	F	Z
N	O	P	V	T	K	O	P	I	W	Q	I	R	S	N
N	E	K	W	U	L	A	C	C	E	N	T	L	N	P
L	J	O	X	R	H	T	A	X	L	Q	E	I	R	E
Y	I	R	N	E	F	Z	D	G	F	O	N	N	Z	Y
H	F	E	Z	E	R	O	E	S	Y	M	U	E	K	G
V	I	P	D	G	I	H	N	F	G	H	T	A	T	N
U	E	B	T	E	H	D	Z	U	B	Y	O	E	Z	O
X	I	S	P	U	R	A	A	N	C	G	K	X	M	A
Q	C	U	D	J	W	P	R	A	C	T	I	C	E	D
A	F	F	R	E	T	T	A	N	D	O	J	L	C	B

1) This is the name of a Polish dance...........................

2) A sudden loud sound (the symbol looks like this ' > ')...........................

3) A virtuosic solo section in a concerto..............................

4) This is an Italian word which translates to mean 'held'...........................

5) A 'night' piece...

6) The symphonic introduction to an opera..........................

7) A vertical line used to divide a musical passage.............. ....

8) This is an Italian word which translates to mean 'hurrying'...................................

9) This German word translates to mean 'song'...............................

10) Something all performing musicians must do before a concert......................

The Note-Naming Quiz

To complete this puzzle you need to name the notes on the staves using the clues below.

1) When you look in the mirror you see

   your ....

   \--- \--- \--- \---

2) This is another name for a taxi ....

   \--- \--- \---

3) When you are tired you go to ....

   \--- \--- \---

4) If you are hungry you like to ....

   \--- \--- \--- \---

5) When your parents say NO you must ....

   \--- \--- \---

6) Sometimes they appear on a
   necklace ....

   \--- \--- \--- \---

7) I cannot hear you. I must be ....

   \--- \--- \--- \---

8) This is a type of meat ....

   \--- \--- \--- \---

9

Beethoven's Blockbuster

I	K	B	L	F	S	K	J	S	L	B	Y	L	A	K
S	V	P	E	U	Q	M	E	C	K	W	R	I	P	J
L	T	N	A	X	Q	I	E	R	O	I	C	A	S	Y
W	Z	B	A	S	L	J	R	X	U	X	H	O	Z	O
A	S	H	P	I	T	A	D	O	R	A	O	V	J	Q
W	B	T	D	M	X	O	I	R	C	L	R	Y	L	K
B	S	Z	C	P	A	Q	R	X	I	S	A	T	F	Y
F	T	V	I	G	D	E	N	A	E	B	L	U	K	R
N	G	O	S	V	E	C	U	H	L	W	K	T	T	A
J	W	M	H	J	M	G	Y	V	U	K	A	G	D	Z
B	A	D	Z	D	W	H	C	I	N	R	F	M	S	Y
H	Z	T	N	V	L	Q	T	H	V	P	X	J	R	U
A	K	C	G	B	Y	Z	D	F	U	A	T	O	S	N
F	N	Y	Q	G	O	V	A	X	A	P	N	A	B	G
B	F	H	E	L	Z	M	I	C	W	P	T	Y	M	O

Beethoven wrote 9 Symphonies. Three of these Symphonies were given special names.
The first task for this puzzle requires you to complete the anagrams below:

Anagrams:	Answers:
INAIPSISMO	....
NADNETA	....
OTESONUST	....
ALTEROMNDO	....
TOISANTO	....
LARLENATOND	....
ELALRGETOT	....
GELIGERO	....

As a clue I will tell you that they are all Italian musical terms.

Once you have the answers to each anagram take the first letter of each answer and put them together
The word you create is the name of one of Beethoven's Symphonies.

Symphony Name ....

To check that your answer is correct try and find
the name of the Symphony in the word search.

Part Two

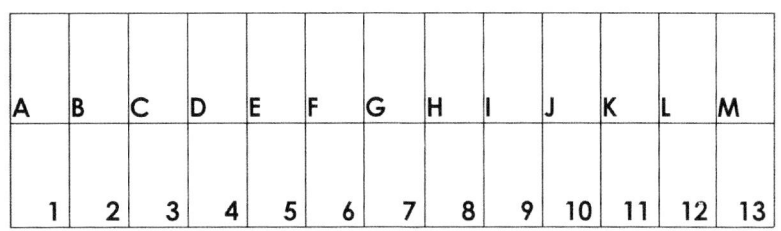

A	B	C	D	E	F	G	H	I	J	K	L	M
1	2	3	4	5	6	7	8	9	10	11	12	13

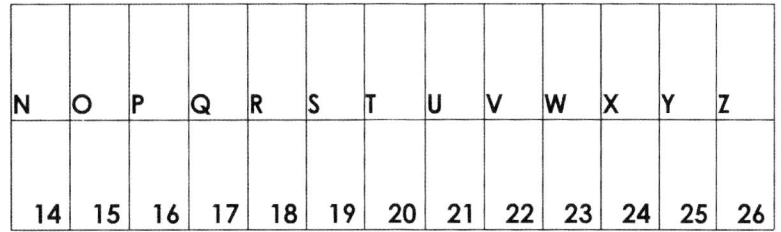

N	O	P	Q	R	S	T	U	V	W	X	Y	Z
14	15	16	17	18	19	20	21	22	23	24	25	26

Beethoven's 3rd Symphony also had a special name.

To work out the name first you need to answer the 6 questions on the next page.

When you have the answers use the table above to convert the answer into a

letter. If you have the answers correct the letters will spell the name of

Beethoven's 3rd Symphony. To check that the name is correct try and find

the name of the Symphony in the word search at the beginning of this puzzle.

Question One: How many mistakes can you find in the melody below? ....

Question Two: How many semiquavers does the following rhythm equal?......................

Question Three: How many quavers does the following rhythm equal?...........................

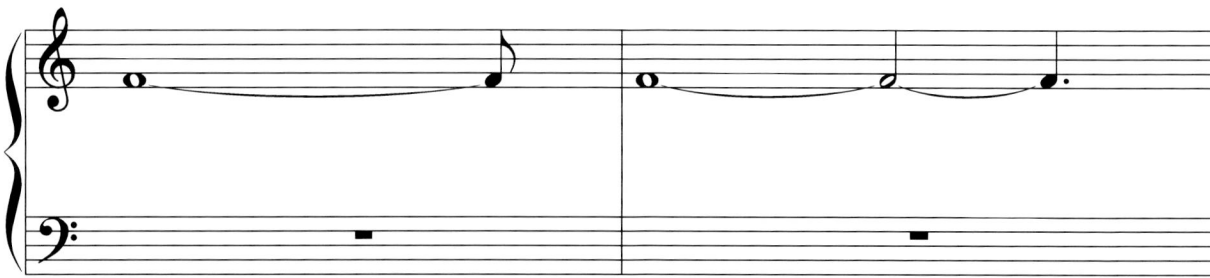

Question Four: The time signature below is incorrect. What should the top number read?...........................

Question Five: How many sharps does F# minor have in the key signature?...........

Question Six: How many Flats does D minor have in the Key signature?..............

This is the final part of the puzzle. By now you should have the names of two of Beethoven's Symphonies; The 6th and the 3rd.

Beethoven's 9th Symphony also had a famous title. To find the name you need to search for it in the word search. If you were successful in finding the other names you should find this one quite quickly. The only clue I will give you is that the name of this Symphony has something to do with singing.

Good Luck !!!!!

The name of Beethoven's 9th Symphony is

The………………………..Symphony

Puccini. Bellini. Rossini.

(three of the Greatest Italian Operatic Composers of the 19th Century)

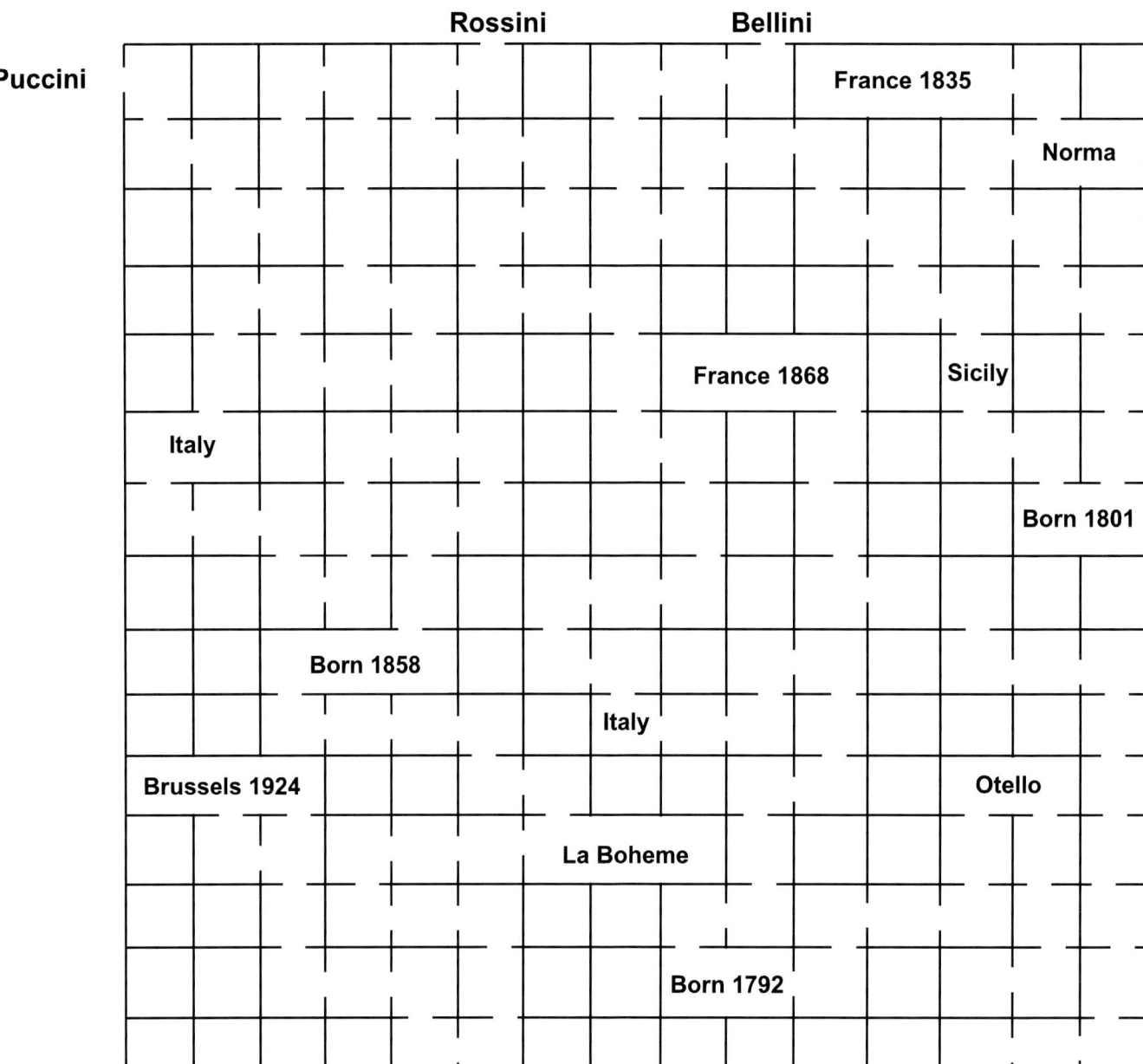

To complete this puzzle you need to answer the questions on the next page

Use this maze to find your answers.

GOOD LUCK.

Please answer the following questions using the maze to help you.

1) In which year was Puccini born? ………………………

2) Which composer wrote the opera 'Otello'? …………………….

3) Who died in Brussels in 1924? ………………………………

4) Which composer was born in Sicily? …………………………

5) Which composer wrote the opera 'La Boheme'? …………………………..

6) Who died in France in 1835? ………………………

7) In which year was Bellini born? …………………………..

8) Which composer was born in 1792? ……………………..

9) How old was Puccini when he died? …………………….

10) Which composer (Puccini, Bellini, or Rossini) lived the longest? …………….

The Real Puzzle

To complete this puzzle you need to do three tasks;
Task One: Use the clues below to find the words hidden in the word search.
Task two: Find your answers in the word search.
Task three: In addition to these words there are two musical terms
hidden in the word search. If you find all the correct answers
you are close to finding the two Italian musical terms.

A	L	E	G	G	I	E	R	O	I	B	E	O	H	D
D	E	N	D	C	A	G	E	K	D	N	B	U	Q	T
L	G	L	O	C	K	E	N	S	P	I	E	L	K	A
J	A	N	D	A	N	T	E	T	H	K	C	G	J	O
G	T	R	I	A	N	G	L	E	F	Z	P	S	C	V
D	O	F	B	I	A	L	M	L	O	M	E	O	I	N
H	N	C	K	R	J	U	F	P	R	Q	F	F	L	U
Z	T	B	T	N	K	Y	G	I	W	T	L	U	N	I
M	P	R	B	E	H	C	Y	R	O	C	T	A	V	E
Z	S	Q	J	N	T	N	E	T	A	I	C	U	P	T
J	A	W	M	Q	O	X	U	N	A	C	O	R	D	A
R	L	E	C	E	P	N	D	V	T	D	S	D	V	X
Y	X	O	S	I	E	U	P	H	O	N	I	U	M	G
F	I	Z	X	T	B	P	C	W	L	E	Y	H	Q	V
A	E	H	K	X	R	M	W	G	Z	J	V	S	W	Y

1) A Brass Instrument...
2) A 'curve' which joins two notes of the same pitch.............................
3) The Italian musical term used to describe the soft pedal on the piano.........
4) Three quavers joined together in simple time...............................
5) An interval of eight notes.................................
6) This Italian musical term translates to mean 'light, delicate'...........................
7) A percussion instrument which has three sides...
8) This Italian musical term translates to mean 'walking pace'...........................
9) The name given to a group of eight instrumentalists................................
10) Another percussion instrument. This one has metal keys ....
11) This short Italian word translates to mean 'Not'......................
12) Indicated by the double bar line..................

The two Italian musical terms are:
a).....................................…
b)...

The Easter Puzzle

Welcome to the Easter Puzzle…

There are three parts to this puzzle:

Part One:

For part one of the puzzle you need to solve the anagrams on the next page using the clues to help you.

Part Two:

For part two of the puzzle you need to try and fit your anagram solutions into the crossword.

Part Three:

If you have completed part two successfully you will discover that the crossword is incomplete. There is a word missing. To solve the puzzle just complete the sentence on the third page and add the missing word to the crossword.

Good luck
and
have fun

Part One:

Anagrams	Solutions	Clues
SGINITMETAREU	…………………………	Can be 'simple' or 'compound'
ECALS	…………………………	Sometimes known as a 'ladder of notes'
AURKAZM	…………………………	A Polish dance
ETI	…………………………	A bend over two notes of the same pitch
CICANEDALT	…………………………	Added sharp, natural or flat in music
TERS	…………………………	You cannot play, but you must count
DIRAT	…………………………	A chord of three notes. (1st, 3rd, 5th)
ELELIGENSR	…………………………	For notes above or below the stave
PUHEONUMI	…………………………	A brass instrument
UIRGTA	…………………………	A stringed instrument
PITRELT	…………………………	Three notes of equal value grouped in 'simple time' to equal the value of two
EONISETM	…………………………	The seventh note of the 'harmonic' minor scale is raised a….?
EOCTRN	…………………………	Another brass instrument
EATSV	…………………………	Is used when writing notes in music
ECTOROCN	…………………………	Large orchestral piece with an important soloist
TIQUNET	…………………………	A group of five instrumentalists
SAIORNLAGC	…………………………	A woodwind instrument
ECODL	…………………………	Italian musical term 'sweetly'
LATANIECB	…………………………	Italian musical term 'singing style'
OALELARTMT	…………………………	Italian musical term 'hammered out'
AONIAPL	…………………………	A keyboard instrument which plays by itself

Part Two

Try and fit the anagram solutions in the crossword below

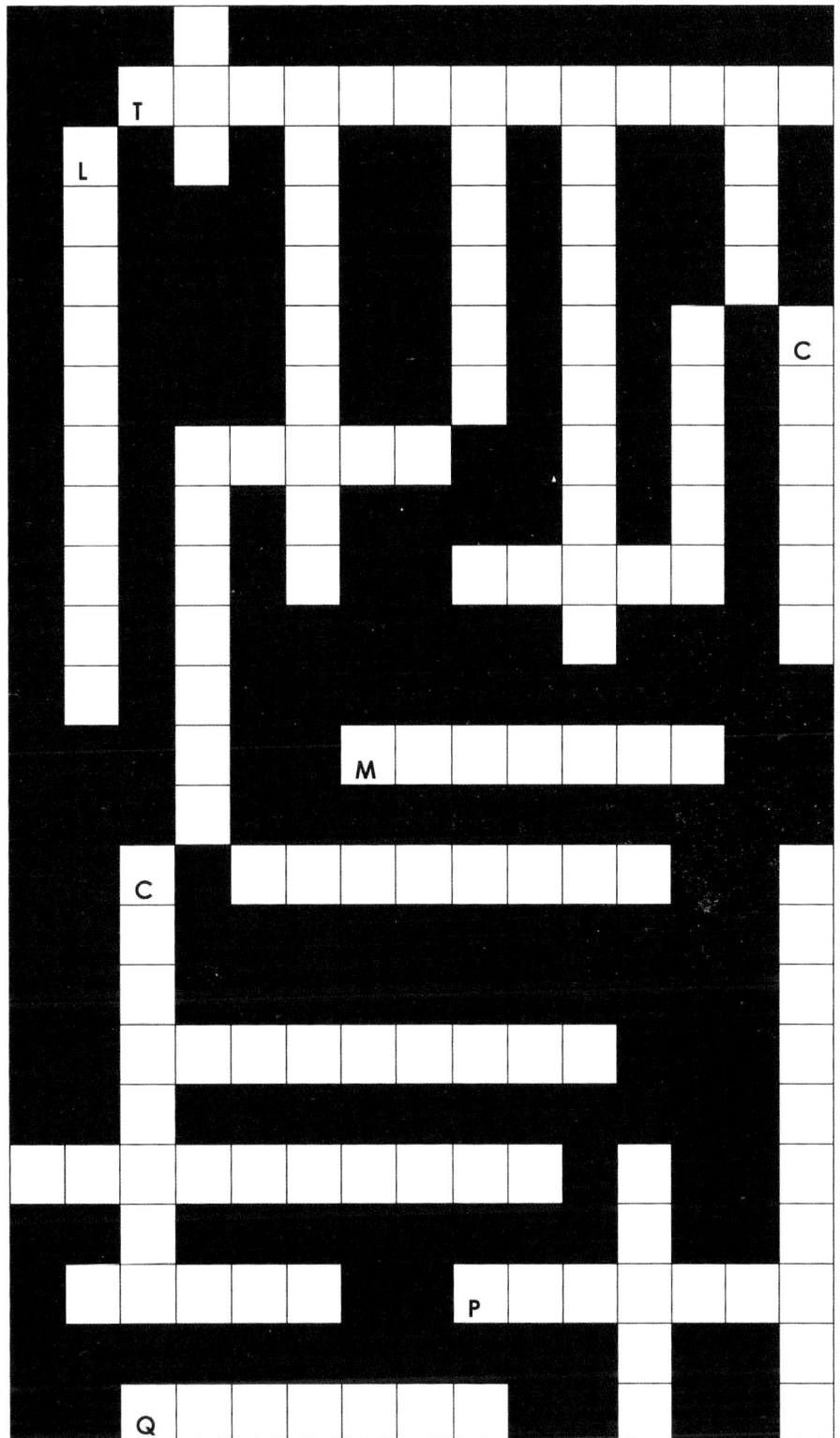

Part Three

To complete the puzzle find the missing word by completing this sentence:

.........................is a type of dance which originates from Argentina

Anagram madness

To complete this puzzle try and solve the following anagrams using the clues provided.

Anagram	clue	solution
LGIEPOLCEKNS	This is a percussion instrument which has metal keys	....
ABUT	A large brass instrument	....
ACOD	Often appears at the end of a piece of music	....
NOBROMET	A long brass instrument	....
LALERGETOT	Lively but slower than Allegro	....
EARTUQT	A group of four instrumentalists	....
SARACAM	This percussion instrument can be shaken	....
PAHR	A stringed instrument which has three sides	....
BANCTALIE	In Italian this word means 'singing style'	....
OFARFETATND	In Italian this word means 'hurrying'	....

The Musical Crossword

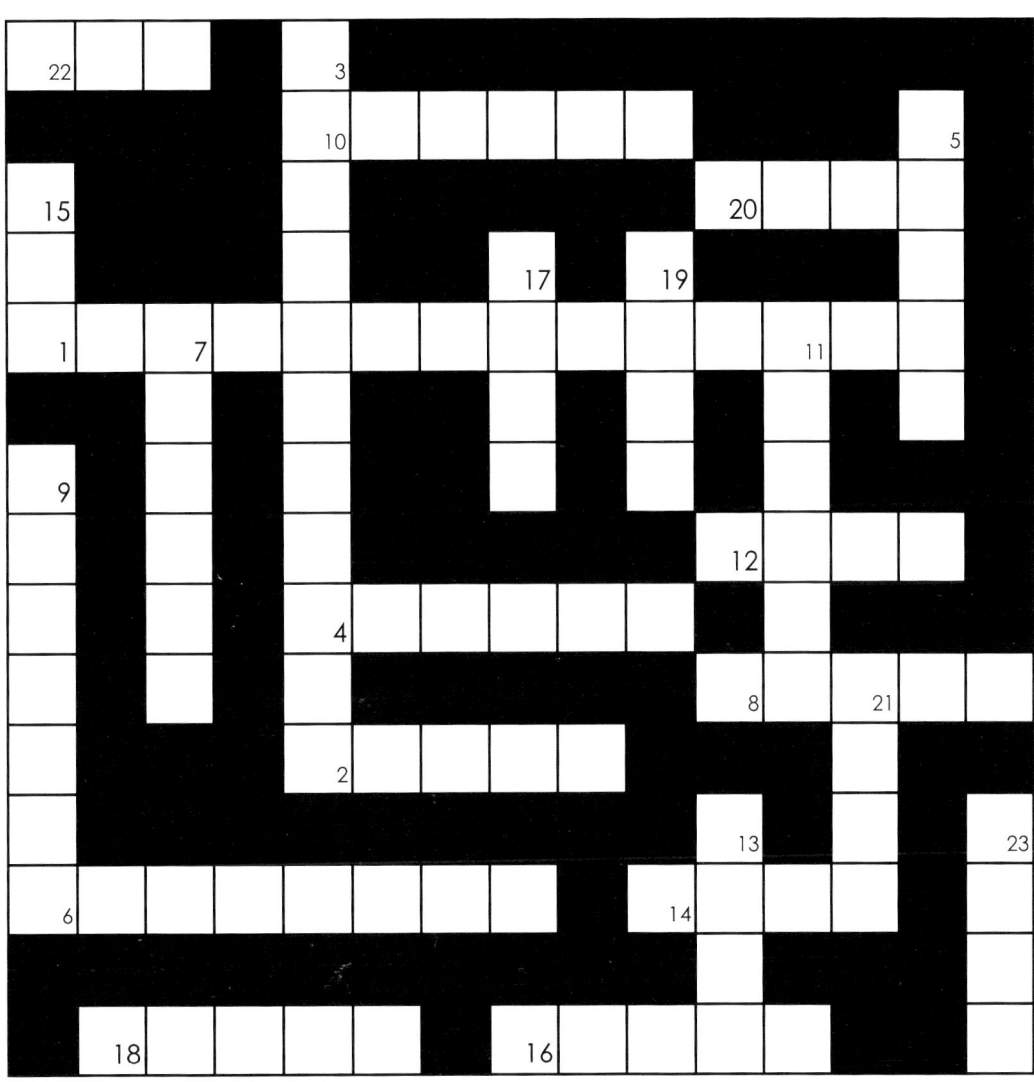

Clues going across

1=A quick note with 3 tails (14)

2=Sweetly (5)

4=Interval of 8 notes (6)

6=Orchestra (8)

8=Slow (5)

10=Sudden loud sound (6)

12=Getting slower (4)

14=Colour and sound (4)

16=Musical instrument, also soft (5)

18=Sign raises the note (5)

20=A note on leger lines in the treble clef (4)

22=A note on leger lines in the bass clef (3)

Clues going down

3=Early keyboard instrument (11)

5=Several notes played together (5)

7= Composer, Austrian 'Cosi Fan Tutti' (6)

9=A violin has 4 of these (6)

11=Very lively (6)

13=Brass instrument (4)

15=Indicated by the double bar line (3)

17=Early violin (4)

19=Another word for melody (4)

21=Written on the stave (4)

23=Can be treble or bass (4)

The Summer Puzzle

Welcome to the summer puzzle. There are three parts to this puzzle….

Part One:

On the next page you will find 17 questions relating to key signatures. Most of the answers require a number but questions 3), 8), and 16) require a word. (note how question 14) is missing)

Part Two:

Once you have completed part one use 'grid A' to convert your answers into letters.
Then use 'grid B' to find out the composer's full surname. Now you need to try and fit the composer's names into the crossword. The numbers in the crossword represent the numbers for each question in part one.

Part Three:

When you have completed part two you will discover that the crossword is incomplete. (question 14) is missing) to find the missing word you need to complete the sentence at the bottom of page two.

Good luck

Part One

Please complete the following questions by adding a number. (except for questions 3), 8) and 16) which require a word). (Question 14)is missing)

Clue	Question	Clue	Question
1) across	D major has ……… sharps	11) across	F minor has ……… flats
2) down	G# minor has ……… sharps	12) across	F major has ……… flat
3) down	C# ……… has 4 sharps	13) down	E minor has ……… sharp
4) across	G minor has ……… flats	15) across	A major has ……… sharp
5) across	E major has ……… sharps	16) down	C major and A minor have ………
6) down	B minor has ……… sharps	17) across	Bb major has ……… flats
7) across	Ab major has ……… flats		
8) across	Db ……… has 5 flats		
9) down	Eb major has ……… flats		
10) across	F# minor has ……… sharps		

Grid A

A	B	C	D	E	F	G
1	2	3	4	5	6	7

Grid B

Chopin	Albeniz	Bernstein	Cage
Delius	Copland	Boccherini	
Donizetti	Alkan	Elgar	
Dvorak	Bach	Beethoven	

23

Part Two

Try and fit the composer's surnames into the crossword

Part Three

To find the answer for 14) down please complete the following sentence:

All minor scales have ....

Lost for words in Italy

To complete this puzzle you need to translate the English musical meanings into Italian and then fit your answers into the crossword.

English musical meanings: Italian translation:

Slow (6)   ....

Hurrying (11)   ....

With fire (5)   ....

Sadly (5)   ....

Sweeetly (5)   ....

Lively (7)   ....

As fast as possible (11)   ....

Walking speed (7)   ....

Go on immediately (7)   ....

With life (animated) (7)   ....

As loud as possible (10)   ....

Voice (4)   ....

Dying away (7)   ....

Delicate (8)   ....

Suddenly (6)   ....

The Numerical Puzzle

Welcome to The Numerical Puzzle…

There are three parts to this puzzle.

Part One:

To complete part one you need to complete the note and rest value equations by adding or subtracting.

Part Two:

When you have completed part one try and find your answers in the number grid. To help you all the correct answers are close together. Use '0' as a space and join the numbers together. If you have the correct answers they will form the shape of another number.

Part Three:

Use the number from part two to complete the sentence…

Good Luck

The Numerical Puzzle

Please complete the following musical equations by adding or subtracting the note and rest values.

Part Two

To complete part two of this puzzle try and find your answers from the musical equations in the number grid below. All the correct answers are close together. If you use '0' to represent a space, join the numbers together and they will form the shape of another number. Use this number to complete the sentence below.

0	5	6	9	12	16	8	13	9	7	26	14	7	6	9
15	45	37	11	8	6	7	9	14	12	5	8	13	16	8
7	6	5	8	9	7	26	9	5	14	8	12	42	39	6
9	13	7	14	18	23	0	2	4	5	7	8	6	7	12
15	32	16	12	9	4	7	6	0	18	21	32	15	9	42
12	16	45	0	8	3	14	9	3	23	48	17	6	34	15
11	14	7	9	6	0	2	0	2	12	43	16	7	38	12
13	9	7	12	7	14	8	6	0	11	0	6	14	12	32
8	14	16	8	14	13	42	9	4	13	21	34	8	6	12
7	0	8	6	14	23	11	5	0	8	7	14	9	6	11
45	12	17	14	6	8	5	19	1	21	32	15	12	7	9
5	7	8	5	9	12	13	6	15	28	14	7	0	13	21
8	17	6	15	42	38	12	15	8	6	5	7	11	10	18
5	6	9	0	20	32	11	0	15	23	7	9	14	6	5
23	13	15	6	9	14	8	5	32	12	14	6	7	9	12

Part Three

To complete this puzzle just answer the following question:

Ludwig Van Beethoven wrote .... complete symphonies

28

Mission Impossible

To complete this puzzle first answer the questions below by writing the word.

When you have all the answers try and find them in the word search, and then......

try and find the three mystery Italian musical terms.

Clue: If you find all of your answers you are close to finding the mystery words.

M	A	L	A	M	B	O	B	O	V	L	V	P	E	U
A	P	L	J	N	Q	V	G	B	O	N	L	T	N	W
R	N	R	U	E	P	R	H	K	M	A	C	U	H	A
T	Q	O	D	C	A	I	Y	U	T	T	Y	Z	A	X
E	K	M	E	L	I	H	X	N	E	U	M	S	R	W
L	E	R	E	O	G	D	E	W	T	R	D	O	M	T
L	A	J	K	D	F	D	T	C	R	A	R	C	O	R
A	R	E	N	S	I	L	F	G	A	L	U	Q	N	Z
T	F	X	G	C	J	A	D	V	C	I	S	B	I	N
O	U	M	C	S	E	I	N	T	H	M	S	X	C	G
L	Q	A	E	H	J	S	Y	T	O	R	I	F	W	G
W	O	D	Z	C	D	S	L	U	R	A	A	F	O	A
B	T	F	U	O	C	O	B	G	D	Y	N	F	I	H
A	C	A	P	P	E	L	L	A	Z	S	X	Z	P	V
N	P	C	K	A	C	M	Y	L	B	Q	H	K	E	J

Italian Musical Terms

a) ....

b) ....

c) ....

1) An added sharp or flat in music is called an ....

2) A change of sharp or flat to create the same pitch is called an .... change

3) A ....sign removes the sharp or flat

4)............................. is a Greek word which translates to mean ' group of four notes' It is used in scales

5) The .... is the technical name for the third note of the scale

6) A bend over two notes of different pitches is called a ....

7) This Italian word translates to mean 'unaccompanied vocal music' (church style) ....

8) This Italian word translates to mean 'hammered out' ....

9) A ....is the Argentinean dance of the gauchos (Argentinean cowboys)

10) The nationality of Igor Stravinsky is ....

Graham's Millennium Puzzle

Can you solve the following equation?

$$X + Y + Z = A - B = 30 \text{ -:- } C = ?$$

Perhaps the puzzles on the following pages can help

Good luck and have fun.

Part One:

Try and solve the anagrams below. The first letter of each correct anagram can be put together to spell the name of a famous Ballet. Who wrote it?

Anagrams		**Solutions**
1) IGANIPAN	(clue: very famous violinist and composer)	…………………
2) RALEG	(clue: English composer. Proms)	…………………
3) AHOKTCIYSVK	(clue: He wrote the 1812 overture)	…………………
4) NOSIRSI	(clue: Barber of Seville opera)	…………………
5) NKONWUN	(clue: nobody new him)	…………………
6) TRCEBUHS	(clue: He wrote the Trout Quintet)	…………………
7) DAHYN	(clue: The 'Surprise' Symphony)	…………………
8) YOLAKD	(clue: His School of singing)	…………………
9) ZIALEBN	(clue: Spanish composer)	…………………

Name of the composer…………………………..

Part Two:

1	2	3	4	5	6	7	8	9	10	11	12	13
A	B	C	D	E	F	G	H	I	J	K	L	M

14	15	16	17	18	19	20	21	22	23	24	25	26
N	O	P	Q	R	S	T	U	V	W	X	Y	Z

Have another look at your completed anagrams from Part One. Use the table above to convert the First letter of each solution into a number.

For example: If the solution was 'Mozart'. Take the first letter which is 'M' and use the table above to convert it into a letter. M = 13.

Once you have done this take the numbers for the FIRST anagram, FIFTH anagram and NINTH anagram.

These numbers can be put into the equation to represent the letters: X + Y+ Z

With these clues you should now be able to work out what A =

X = …………………….…

Y = ………………….……

Z = ……………….………

Part Three:

For this Part of the Puzzle you need to study the musical passage above. The bottom number in the time signature is wrong. What should the number be?

The answer can be used to represent the letter B in the equation.

B = ...

Part Four:

To find the next clue in the equation you need to complete the following paragraph by adding the missing words.

I know that A MAJOR has…………………sharps and G MAJOR has only………. If I were to add my two answers together I would have …………sharps and I would be able to name the MAJOR key-signature whose RELATIVE MINOR is…………………If I took the RELATIVE MAJOR of the answer above……………..and subtracted it from the key signature of D MAJOR. Of course D MAJOR has………sharps, I would have the answer for my next clue in this puzzle.

Once you have the answer you can include it in the equation to represent the letter C.

C = …………………

Part Five:

If you have reached this page, congratulations. You have reached the last hurdle.

The final part of this puzzle involves answering the following question.

How many complete Symphonies did Dimitri Shostakovich write?

To find the answer to the question all you need to do is put all the clues together and solve the equation.

$$X + Y + Z = A - B = 30 \div C = ?$$

----- + ----- + ----- = ----- - ----- = 30 -:- ----- = -----

When you have solved the equation just complete the question.

Dimitri Shostakovich wrote ………. complete Symphonies.

The Treble Clef crossword

Clues going across

1=Expression marks in Music (8)

3=He wrote the 'Surprise' Symphony (5)

6=Percussion instrument (7)

7=Musical word which means 'speed' (5)

9=Name given to Beethoven's
    6th Symphony (8)

11=Hungarian pianist and composer (5)

13=Italian term 'with movement' (7)

16=A musical ornament (4)

17=Another percussion instrument (4)

19=A woodwind instrument (4)

20=This German word means 'song' (6)

21=Another word for 'melody' (4)

22=A Brass instrument (4)

24=Opera by Montiverdi (5)

25=A Tonic Triad (3)

Clues going down

2=An abbreviation indicating a repeat back to the beginning (2)

4=Russian composer (12)

5=This Italian term means 'sadly' (5)

8=This Italian term means 'in the style of unaccompanied vocal music (9)

10=Religious choral work (8)

12=Italian word and sometimes a musical sign which means 'held' (6)

14=An Italian term which means 'in a singing style' (9)

15=Indicated by the double bar line (3)

18=A very early woodwind instrument (8)

23=This abbreviation indicates to the performer to use their right hand (2)

Can you solve the following anagrams?

1) MYRHTH ………………………… (clue: you need to count)

2) TERTMUP ………………………… (clue: don't blow your own…)

3) CANUROAD ………………………… (clue: relates to the piano)

4) EGNLIART ………………………… (clue: three sides)

5) COLED ………………………… (clue: sugar is very….in Italy)

6) OCELEARNADC ………………………… (clue: are you getting faster?)

7) TORCHETC ………………………… (clue: In 4/4 there are four)

8) NOHR ………………………… (clue: made of Brass)

9) OLELRGA ………………………… (clue: lively)

10) RAEVQUSMIEDIME ………………… (clue: that was quick)

The Musical Term word search

To complete this puzzle translate the English musical terms below into Italian and then try and find your answers in the word search

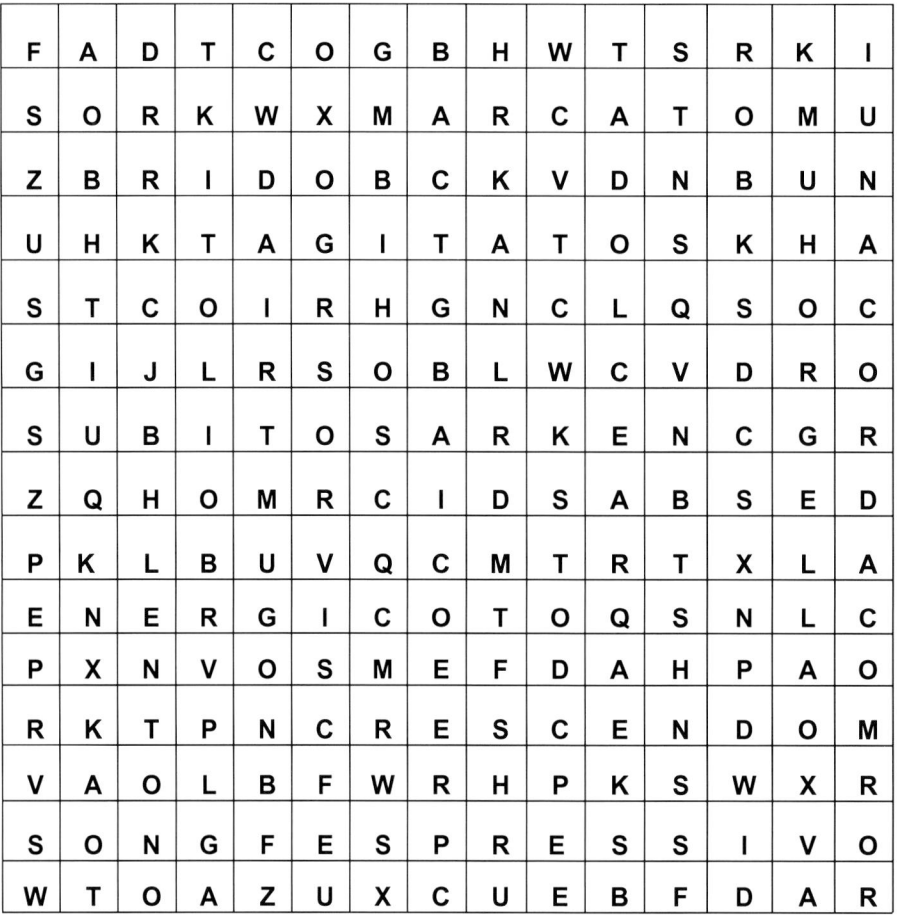

F	A	D	T	C	O	G	B	H	W	T	S	R	K	I
S	O	R	K	W	X	M	A	R	C	A	T	O	M	U
Z	B	R	I	D	O	B	C	K	V	D	N	B	U	N
U	H	K	T	A	G	I	T	A	T	O	S	K	H	A
S	T	C	O	I	R	H	G	N	C	L	Q	S	O	C
G	I	J	L	R	S	O	B	L	W	C	V	D	R	O
S	U	B	I	T	O	S	A	R	K	E	N	C	G	R
Z	Q	H	O	M	R	C	I	D	S	A	B	S	E	D
P	K	L	B	U	V	Q	C	M	T	R	T	X	L	A
E	N	E	R	G	I	C	O	T	O	Q	S	N	L	C
P	X	N	V	O	S	M	E	F	D	A	H	P	A	O
R	K	T	P	N	C	R	E	S	C	E	N	D	O	M
V	A	O	L	B	F	W	R	H	P	K	S	W	X	R
S	O	N	G	F	E	S	P	R	E	S	S	I	V	O
W	T	O	A	Z	U	X	C	U	E	B	F	D	A	R

English musical term   Italian translation

1) Agitated   ....

2) Hurrying   ....

3) Lively   ....

4) Sweetly   ....

5) Getting louder   ....

6) Very loud   ....

7) With energy   ....

8) With expression   ....

9) Slow   ....

10) Marked, accented   ....

11) Suddenly   ....

12) Use the soft pedal   ....

The word search with a difference

To complete this puzzle there are three tasks:

Task one: Try and find the six Italian musical terms in the word search.

Task two: Answer questions 7-12 by writing the correct word.

Task three: Try and find your answers in the word search.

A	Q	L	S	G	O	C	Y	E	N	T	F	W	N	P
E	H	B	C	H	J	U	I	M	Q	D	O	L	C	E
F	C	R	E	S	C	E	N	D	O	V	K	S	H	U
I	B	A	V	X	C	F	G	B	D	J	C	G	O	H
P	K	A	D	K	I	N	J	X	M	Y	O	L	R	D
E	I	D	F	U	O	C	O	L	T	O	Z	Q	D	P
R	N	Z	R	N	C	W	M	S	L	E	G	A	T	O
H	T	I	T	A	T	U	A	D	V	Y	E	R	W	Z
U	E	M	F	C	A	L	L	E	G	R	O	B	X	O
O	R	T	K	O	V	I	O	L	C	J	N	A	C	V
L	V	L	G	R	E	I	R	Y	F	Q	A	K	P	Z
H	A	K	B	D	U	G	M	S	X	E	E	W	J	R
N	L	T	P	A	N	D	A	N	T	E	W	T	D	M
J	S	D	I	U	Z	V	F	C	W	G	N	L	H	Y
R	V	Q	T	R	I	A	D	V	B	P	Q	X	S	O

Italian musical terms:

1) Fuoco
2) Una corda
3) Crescendo
4) Dolce
5) Interval
6) Triad

Please answer the following questions:

7) This Italian word translates to mean 'smoothly'...........................

8) This is an early stringed instrument.......................

9) This Italian word translates to mean 'slow, walking pace'.................

10) This word is used to describe an interval of eight notes...................

11) A 'cluster' of notes.........................

12) This Italian word translates to mean 'lively'.............................

39

General Knowledge word search

S	Y	M	P	H	O	N	Y	X	W	C	D	N	R	X
D	R	Q	N	Z	P	R	K	L	O	A	E	O	S	C
B	C	O	U	L	E	G	E	R	L	I	N	E	T	R
A	N	W	X	A	V	A	B	R	D	W	D	X	V	E
T	C	S	U	R	V	M	E	F	S	X	O	N	U	S
A	P	C	Q	F	E	E	T	C	R	V	M	K	W	C
V	C	E	I	N	B	A	R	D	C	R	I	O	T	E
F	K	U	S	D	A	D	I	S	T	A	N	C	E	N
O	N	V	C	B	E	O	R	C	E	B	A	D	U	D
U	K	R	T	S	V	N	O	P	Q	X	N	R	T	O
R	S	O	F	I	V	E	T	V	S	K	T	M	P	Z
N	A	C	F	E	G	R	T	A	S	N	J	L	O	N
P	R	Q	T	S	V	X	B	C	L	R	H	N	P	J
K	S	T	D	O	L	C	E	N	V	L	K	O	I	S
O	X	V	W	B	R	N	V	S	K	V	O	X	B	D

Try and complete the sentences below by inserting the missing word.
To check if your answers are correct try and find the words
in the word search.

1) The difference between Simple and Compound time signatures .
Simple time signatures relate to the crotchet.
Compound time signatures relate to the...

2) The 'Stave' consists of ....lines.

3) An 'Interval' is the ....between two notes.

4) The..............................is the technical name for the fifth note of the scale.

5) An..................................is the name given to an added sharp or flat in music.

6) ....is an Italian musical term which translates to mean 'sweetly'

7) ....is an Italian musical term which translates to mean 'getting louder'

8) There are..........................instruments in a string quartet.

9) A.......................................is a large orchestral piece.

10) Notes written above or below the stave may use a ....

The Composer Nationality Quiz

Try and find the countries opposite in the word search

Countries:

T	B	A	M	E	R	I	C	A	R	T	V	O	K	R
S	U	V	R	N	B	C	A	V	X	H	W	J	M	O
P	K	N	S	T	R	V	X	C	D	U	E	G	A	R
F	J	K	O	R	G	E	R	M	A	N	Y	X	V	N
T	R	B	S	V	U	N	O	R	M	G	K	J	X	R
C	Z	E	C	H	O	S	L	O	V	A	K	I	A	V
B	R	N	A	D	N	O	S	X	T	R	C	T	U	E
V	J	G	K	A	P	R	F	I	H	Y	I	A	S	A
H	A	L	P	N	C	E	I	S	A	D	R	L	T	V
F	R	A	N	C	E	H	J	A	N	O	K	Y	R	S
Z	J	N	F	I	C	S	P	A	I	N	Z	C	I	X
L	O	D	V	A	P	O	L	A	N	D	B	R	A	C
Q	O	C	L	D	R	N	O	R	W	A	Y	F	D	H
M	E	A	Y	P	I	R	J	V	K	E	S	X	I	W
B	Z	N	S	F	U	B	O	H	E	M	I	A	G	T

Countries:

Bohemia

Norway

England

Czechoslovakia

Germany

Austria

Hungary

Italy

France

Finland

Russia

Poland

Spain

America

Japan

Where do these composers come from?

Gustav Mahler ....

Edward Grieg ....

Ludwig Van Beethoven ....

Wolfgang Amadeus Mozart ....

Antonin Dvorak ....

Bela Bartok ....

Claude Debussy ....

Giacomo Puccini ....

Igor Stravinsky ....

Jean Sibelius ....

Frederic Chopin ....

George Gershwin ....

Edward Elgar ....

Joaquin Rodrigo ....

Toru Takemitsu ....

Composer Nationalities

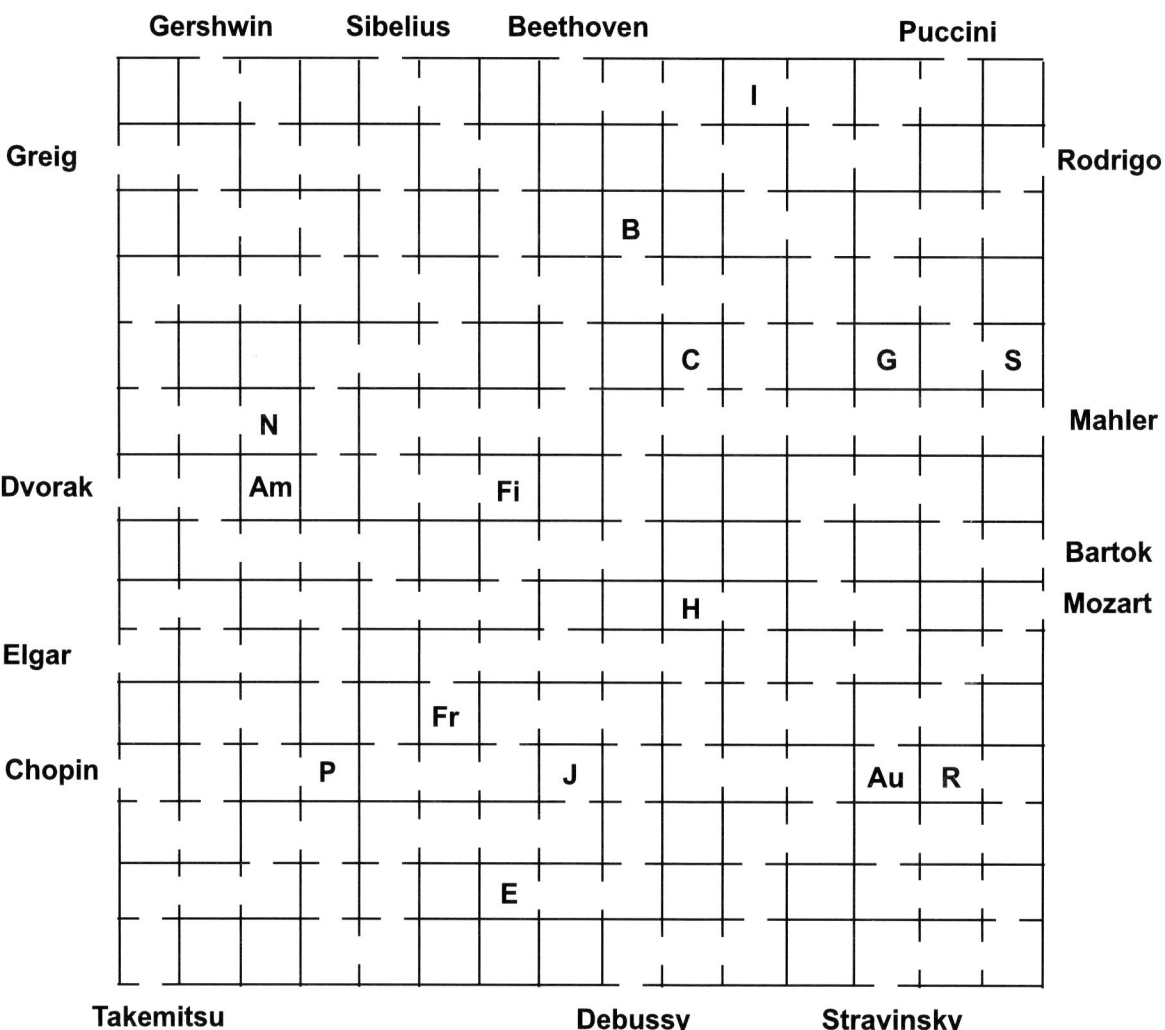

To find out which countries each composer comes from you need to follow the gaps in the maze. Enter the maze from the gap relating to each composer and follow the trail. When you reach a letter (or letters) check them against the first letters of each country on the previous page and complete the sentences